British Road Tunnels – An Introduction

MARK CHATTERTON

First published in 2016 by Hadleigh Books as an ebook

This book is also available in the following formats:-

Mobi version for Amazon Kindle ISBN 978-1-910811-54-2
PDF file for Personal Computer ISBN 978-1-910811-56-6

www.hadleighbooks.co.uk

MARK CHATTERTON

Front cover:

The northern portal to the Queensway Tunnel on the A38 in Central Birmingham, looking southwards.

CONTENTS

INTRODUCTION

As someone who has been visiting and photographing road tunnels for well over ten years now, I have gained plenty of information about this particular aspect of British engineering. It has been a fascinating journey from the far north west of Scotland down to Cornwall in the south west. As no other books have been published on Britain's road tunnels in this way to my knowledge, I have taken the liberty to write this short introductory book.

It gives some basic information about the various types of road tunnels that are found in Britain and the methods used to build them. A much larger book on road tunnels by me was published by Amberley Books in 2020 which goes into greater detail about this interesting engineering phenomenon.

.

THE DEFINTION OF A ROAD TUNNEL

For the purposes of this book, I would define a road tunnel as one that has been built for a motor vehicle - especially a car - to travel through with ease. It should be on a public road and not within a car park or part of a private building.

As to what constitutes a tunnel, that is a harder question to answer. Most people define a tunnel as an underground passage which is longer than it is wide. Some over bridges could meet this definition, so I would say that for a road tunnel to be included in this book, it should be a least ten yards long. It could also go under a building, airport runway, railway embankment, as well as under the ground.

The Department of Transport has their own definition of what constitutes a road tunnel and this includes having a minimum length of 150 metres (or 164 yards). However, each person has their view of what constitutes a road tunnel, but generally speaking most people know a road tunnel when they see one. The debate is bound to continue......

THE DIFFERENT METHODS OF

CONSTRUCTING ROAD TUNNELS

When building a tunnel, whether road or rail, or anything else for that matter, most members of the general public seem to think that it is just a case of digging or cutting a hole through rock or soil until you come out at the other end. However, this is just one of several methods of constructing a tunnel in the twenty first century. I will now look at the four main methods of tunnel construction in the UK.

Bored

This is when a tunnel is bored through the earth using a special cutting machine built for the job, such as the various tunnels in London's Crossrail Project. However, in the 19th and early 20th centuries, most tunnels were built by thousands of labourers armed with just picks and shovels. In some cases, gunpowder or dynamite was added into the mix to help get through some of the harder types of rock such as granite.

Here is and example of a bored tunnel:-

The Cuilfail Tunnel in Lewes, East Sussex on the opposite page, takes the A26 away from the town centre and under Cliffe Hill, to join up with the A27, which runs to the south of Lewes. Cliffe Hill is a chalk based earthwork, which was cut through with boring machines in 1978-79. The tunnel was opened to the public in 1980. It is a typical example of a road tunnel created by the boring method. The giant "snail" on the roundabout is in fact a sculpture of an ammonite, examples of which were found during the tunnel's construction. The photograph shows the western entrance to the tunnel.

Other examples of bored road tunnels include:-

The Clyde Tunnel, Glasgow – opened 1963/4
The Gibraltar Hill Tunnel, Monmouth – opened 1967
The Mersey Tunnel (also known as the Queensway Tunnel), Liverpool – opened 1934

Cut and Cover

Possibly, the most common method of tunnel construction in Britain today. Basically, a trench is dug which is open to the elements. Then a roof or cover is placed over the top of the trench to convert it into a tunnel.

An example of a cut and cover tunnel:-

The Hatfield Tunnel on the A1 Motorway goes under the Galleria Shopping Centre in Hatfield and is a prime example of a road tunnel built by the "cut and cover" method.

It has two twin bore tunnels of three lanes, plus a hard shoulder and is one the widest road tunnels in Great Britain. It was opened in 1986. The photo is looking north with the large glass dome of the Galleria centre above it.

Other examples of cut and cover tunnels:-

Fore Street Tunnel, Edmonton, London – opened 1998
Hangar Lane Tunnel, Ealing, London – opened 1960
Holmesdale Tunnel, M25, Hertfordshire – opened 1984

New Austrian Method

This was first developed in the 1960s in Austria. Basically, it is the same as boring, but immediately quick drying concrete is sprayed all around the edges of the cut hole to stabilise the rock above and around it. Plus, a combination of steel ribs, rock bolts and wire mesh may also be used, with constant monitoring of the strata conditions. The only example of this method of tunnel construction in Britain is the Southwick Tunnel, near Brighton in West Sussex.

Opposite is the northern portal of Southwick Tunnel looking east. It is situated on the A27 to the west of Brighton in West Sussex and cuts through a chalk escarpment, which is part of the South Downs National Park. It was opened in 1996 and is 490 metres or 1608 feet in length.

It is the only example of a road tunnel built using this method in the UK. However, the railway line connecting Heathrow Airport to London Paddington also used this construction method when several tunnels were built underneath the airport.

Immersed Tube

This method is for tunnels which go under water. A trench is made along the riverbed, then a series of concrete tubes, which are built elsewhere are floated along the river and lowered into place. The remaining space in the trench is filled in and the riverbed reinstated.

An example of a road tunnel built using an immersed tube

The Conwy Tunnel in North Wales, on the A55 North Wales Express Way, looking west. It is an example of a road tunnel using the immersed tube method, with cut and cover sections at each entrance. It takes the A55 under the River Conwy and past the small town of Conwy, greatly reducing the traffic jams which occurred there in the summer months. It is one of the few road tunnels to have been opened by Queen Elizabeth II.

Other examples of immersed tube road tunnels are:-

The Medway Tunnel, Chatham, Kent – opened 1996

The Tyne Tunnel (Second Tunnel) – opened 2011

THE OLDEST AND NEWEST ROAD TUNNELS

The oldest road tunnel that is still open to motor traffic in the twenty-first century, is the Beaminster Tunnel or Horn Hill Tunnel on the A3066 in Dorset (pictured below). It was first opened in 1832, before any railway tunnels had ever been built. It carried a toll road underneath a hill, Horn Hill, which is situated to the north of Beaminster in Dorset.

The photo on the left shows the northern portal of the Beaminster Tunnel on the A3066 in Dorset. Note how narrow the carriageway is and how high the roof is. It has been repaired at various times during the past fifty or so years due to various collapses of the soil above the tunnel. The collapses occurred in 1968, 2009 and 2012.

Other old road tunnels over a hundred years old include:-
Blackwall Tunnel (western bore) – opened 1897
Charmouth Tunnel, Dorset – opened 1832, closed 1991, but reopened in 2010 as a shooting range - see below
Reigate Tunnel, Surrey – opened 1823. This was the first ever road tunnel in Britain and carried traffic until the 1970s. It is still used by pedestrians.
Rotherhithe Tunnel, London – opened 1908

The newest road tunnel in Great Britain at the time of writing is in Coventry, carrying the inner ring road below an area of green space. It is situated between the town centre and the railway station and is called the Greyfriars Green Tunnel by locals. It was first opened to traffic in Spring 2015.

The eastern portal of the Greyfriars Green Tunnel in Coventry, looking west. Note the cones still in place shortly after its opening in 2015.

THE LONGEST AND SHORTEST ROAD TUNNELS IN BRITAIN

The longest road tunnel in Britain is the Mersey Tunnel between Liverpool and Birkenhead in North West England, which goes under the River Mersey. That was the name that is was known by for many years, but with the opening of a second tunnel under the river Mersey in 1971, it was properly designated as the "Queensway Tunnel" to distinguish it from the other tunnel under the river Mersey, between Liverpool and Wallasey, which is called the "Kingsway Tunnel". It is also the longest road tunnel of all that goes under water, beating its sister tunnel – the Wallasey Tunnel – by half a mile.

Locally the two Mersey tunnels are known as the "Birkenhead Tunnel" and the "Wallasey Tunnel" as these are the two destinations they go to on the other side of the river Mersey from Liverpool.

The tunnel is actually 3237 metres (2 miles) in length and has two other exits – one on each side of the river. The Liverpool exit comes out by the Liver Building and the waterfront, whilst the Birkenhead exit was closed in 1965, but it is still used as a service tunnel.

A view of the Liverpool entrance/exit of the Queensway Tunnel, with the ornate entrance, complete with lime green lamp posts on either side. The tunnel is unusual in that traffic flows both ways with no barrier or separate tunnel between the two routes.

Heavy goods vehicles are banned from using the tunnel. It does not have a designated road number and has its own dedicated police force. Note the statue of King George V to the left of the tunnel.

It was opened by King George V on 18th July 1934 and involved 1,700 men working on its construction. Of these, seventeen were killed during its construction and a memorial to them can be found on the Georges Dock Building in Liverpool. Also there is an original toll booth sited here. It is also the only road tunnel in Great Britain where you can have a guided tour of it. www.merseytunnels.co.uk/noss/html/tunnel _tour.php

The longest road tunnel under land in Great Britain is the Hindhead Tunnel on the A3 in Surrey. At a length of 1.14 miles/1.83 kilometres, it goes under a piece of land known as the Devils Punch Bowl and was opened in 2011. It has two two-lane bores and was constructed via the boring method.

Its opening has cut down the journey time from London to Portsmouth by at least fifteen minutes in most cases. This is because traffic had to go around the edge of the Devil's Punch Bowl escarpment with a 30 mph speed limit and tailbacks were a frequent occurrence. That piece of road has now reverted back to countryside, with no sign of its previous use.

The entrance to the southern portal of the Hindhead Tunnel in Surrey, looking northwards. It has a variable speed limit, with a maximum of 70 mph and has state of the art lighting, air conditioning and fire escape tunnels meeting current EU safety regulations, which were in place when it was constructed.

The shortest road tunnel in Great Britain is possibly the one pictured below. It is situated near the town of Kirkintilloch, north east of Glasgow. It is wide enough to take cars but has a low height which stops vans and lorries passing through it. It is approximately 10 yards/9.1metres in length and only 1.3 metres in height. It goes under the Glasgow and Edinburgh Canal.

Like most minor tunnels in Britain, this tunnel doesn't have a designated name and is not even on a numbered road. It can be found just off the B8023, near Kirkintilloch in Scotland.

BRITISH ROAD TUNNELS – AN INTRODUCTION

ROAD TUNNELS ON MAIN ROADS AND MOTORWAYS

This section looks at tunnels found on Britain's major roads and motorways.

Surprisingly there are very few road tunnels on Britain's motorways, with less than ten in fact. The majority are situated in the South East of England.

The Bell Common Tunnel (opposite), on the M25 in Essex is one of two road tunnels on the M25. (The other one being the Holmesdale Tunnel in Hertfordshire). It is also one of the busiest road tunnels in Great Britain with over fifty million vehicles passing through it each year. It is situated under part of Epping Forest, which meant that a tunnel rather than a cutting had to be built here. There is a cricket pitch belonging to the Foresters Cricket Club, directly above the tunnel.

The Bell Common Tunnel in Essex looking west on the anti-clockwise carriageway of the M25. Note the sign naming the tunnel with the length in yards as opposed to metres.

Other motorway tunnels include:-

Hatfield Tunnel – A1(M)
Holmesdale Tunnel, near Cheshunt - M25
Lofthouse Interchange Tunnel – M1/M62
Woodhouse Tunnel, Leeds – A57(M)

There are around thirty road tunnels on Britain's A roads, most of them on dual carriageways and many of them are situated in London and the South East. As such, these are all named and most of them have signs with their names on near their entrances, as well as a red triangle with a tunnel sign nearby.

The Fore Street Tunnel opposite is situated on the A604 road, better known as the North Circular in North London. It takes the A604 under the A10 coming out of London and so avoids a bottle neck that would occur. It was built by the cut and cover method and opened in 1998.

The picture above shows the Fore Street Tunnel, North London looking west along the A604 dual carriageway. Note the yellow "sentry box" just before the tunnel starts.

Other main road tunnels include:-

Eltham Tunnel, SE London – A2
George Green Tunnel, Wanstead – A12
Penmaenbach Tunnels, North Wales – A55
Saltash Tunnel, Cornwall – A38

TOWN CENTRE AND SHOPPING CENTRE ROAD TUNNELS

This section looks at some of the tunnels found in our town centres and in particular those that go underneath shopping centres.

Most of the road tunnels found in city centres are on A roads, but many of them are unknown to the general public, apart from locals who use them. They are found in London, Birmingham, Newcastle, Coventry, Stirling, Leeds, Glasgow and Dundee. A prime example of this category is the often called Queensway Tunnel in Birmingham. (see opposite)

The Great Charles Street Queensway Tunnel
in central Birmingham to give it its full
name, takes the A38 underneath the A4400
Inner Ring Road and is situated just to the
west of Birmingham city centre. It is one of
three major road tunnels in central
Birmingham.

In city centres there are also road tunnels under some of Britain's shopping centres. Due to the large size of the shopping centres, it was considered easier to build them over existing roads and so create an artificial tunnel rather than fill in the road. They are all open to pedestrians as well as road traffic. Examples of these types of road tunnel can be found in Inverness, Stirling, Southampton, Bristol and Aylesbury.

The A308 Horse Fair Road passes under the Bentall Centre in Kingston-upon-Thames, Surrey, creating an artificial tunnel.

AIRPORT AND RAILWAY STATION ROAD TUNNELS

In this section we look at the various road tunnels found at airports and in and around railway stations.

There are several airports in Britain where there are road tunnels which go under the runways and buildings of these airports. These include Heathrow, Gatwick, Leeds-Bradford, Manchester and Exeter airports. Most are open to the general public, but there are some road tunnels which are airside only and shut to the general public, including ones at Heathrow and Gatwick Airports.

The road tunnel at Luton Airport looking towards the south and Luton Airport Parkway railway station. It takes the A1081 road from the airport terminal under one of the runways and on towards the M1. Note the coned off left side of the tunnel.

When railway lines were first built in Victorian times in towns and cities, land was scarce. So many of these were built on embankments in towns high above the built up areas they went through. Carrying several tracks at once, it was inevitable that tunnels would be built underneath them. In London two stations stand out which have numerous road tunnels underneath them. These are Waterloo and London Bridge.

However, there are road tunnels under railway lines in many other parts of the country including Bristol, Manchester, Newcastle, York and Leeds.

Here is an example of a road tunnel underneath a railway station. This one is at the southern end of Bristol Temple Meads railway station. The tunnel carries Cattle Market Road under the southern end of the station. Since this photograph was taken the road has been realigned and is now one-way only. There are several other road tunnels under Bristol's railway lines, mainly to the north of the station.

OTHER ROAD TUNNELS

In this section we look at other road tunnels which do not fit into the previous categories.

There are plenty of these road tunnels situated all over Britain. Some are former railway tunnels, whilst some are where motorways meet each other. Here are two unusual examples.

The road tunnel opposite is found in the northern seaside town of Blackpool and goes underneath the Pleasure Beach complex in the south of the town. It is on Watson Road and connects the main road which goes along the sea front known as the Promenade with Lytham Road.

It was built as far back as 1932, two years earlier than the more well-known Mersey Tunnel, fifty miles to the south. It is unusual in that at the time of writing you were able to park your car in the tunnel, which is quite rare for a road tunnel. (You can see the author's car parked in the photo on the left hand side of the road!)

This photo of a road tunnel in London is probably the most unusual road tunnel of all. It is found near Canary Wharf in East London. It is called Westferry Circus and is a double-decked roundabout which carries the A1206 north out of the Isle of Dogs, intersecting with other minor roads.

What is unusual is that it is both a surface and an underground roundabout, with the underground section effectively being a tunnel, even though it is round and not straight! It has four entrances/exits and was used by boy racers for a time until the local police stopped this.

BRITISH ROAD TUNNELS – AN INTRODUCTION

Another type of road tunnel found in Great Britain is a toll road tunnel. Many of them having charged a toll ever since they were built, the idea being that the money coming in from the tolls would eventually pay for the cost of building the tunnel.

You used to pay your toll at a toll booth on entering or exiting the tunnel from the comfort of your car. However, this system caused long queues, so nowadays a camera reads the vehicle number plate of the vehicle as it passes a camera and the driver pays on line via a website.

Examples of toll road tunnels include the two Mersey tunnels in Liverpool, the Tyne Tunnel in Newcastle and the Dartford Tunnels in Kent.

The entrance to the original Dartford Tunnel on the Kent side of the River Thames going north. This is the west tunnel which was the first of the two Dartford Tunnels to be opened in 1963. It was originally a two way tunnel, but after a few years it was deemed necessary to build a second tunnel, which was finally opened in 1980. Note the air vent in the upper centre of the picture.

Underpasses

When is a tunnel not a tunnel? When it is an underpass! They are called underpasses by the local authority/Department of Transport because they are not long enough to make the necessary 150 metre length that officially makes them a tunnel, according to their definition. Clearly an underpass is longer inside than a bridge or over bridge, but still shorter than a typical road tunnel.

A good example of an underpass tunnel is the one in Leicester pictured opposite.

Other examples include the ones at Croydon, Euston and Blackfriars. Please note these are all in the London area.

The photograph above shows the Southgates Underpass in Leicester looking north during rush hour. This is situated on Vaughan Way to the west of the city centre and takes the A594 under the A47. It was built to ease congestion where a north-south route met an east-west route near the city centre of Leicester.

ROAD TUNNELS NOT OPEN TO THE PUBLIC

This section included private road tunnels which the general public cannot access and former road tunnels which are no longer in use by road traffic.

In Great Britain there are several road tunnels which are in still used by road vehicles, but which are not open to the general public.

Examples of these include the Pinnock Tunnel in Cornwall, the Heathrow Airport Cargo Tunnel and the Channel Tunnel. The Channel Tunnel has a service road in the centre of it between the two rail tunnels, only open to Channel tunnel staff who drive specially adopted vehicles along it.

Another example of a road tunnel which is closed to the general public is the one below at Gatwick Airport.

This double tunnel on Northgate Road at Gatwick Airport, Surrey has the right hand tunnel open to the public, but the left hand tunnel is behind a high security fence and only open to airline personnel. This is known as being "Airside".

There are also some road tunnels that have been closed over the years, perhaps due a new road being built nearby, or because they were no longer suitable to carry road traffic.

The best example of a closed road tunnel is the one near Charmouth in Dorset, pictured opposite.

Other examples include the Park Tunnel in Nottingham and the Birkenhead Docks exit tunnel leading to the Queensway Tunnel in Birkenhead.

The photograph above shows the entrance to the so called "Charmouth Tunnel" in Dorset. It was originally opened in 1832 as a means to get past a high hill on the Charmouth to Axminster Road, the A35. However, the tunnel was closed in 1991 due to a new road being built nearby to help speed up traffic on the A35. It lay derelict for several years before being turned into an indoor rifle range.

FUTURE ROAD TUNNELS

There are several possible tunnels in the planning stages or are they just a thought in some council planning officer's head!

Here are some of them:-

Silvertown Tunnel. This will be yet another crossing of the River Thames in London. The tunnel would be sited to the east of the Greenwich Dome and cross the Thames to Silvertown on the north bank from the Blackwall Tunnel approach road in the south. It is planned to be operational by 2025.

Stonehenge Tunnel. This is a long running tunnel saga with different proposals in the years 1995, 2002, 2005 and 2013. The idea is to re-route the A303 under the World Heritage site of Stonehenge in Wiltshire with a 1.3 km tunnel.

Thames Gateway Tunnel. This would go under the River Thames about five miles to the east of the Dartford Tunnel. It would join the M25 in Essex to the M2 in Kent via a tunnel crossing, probably between East Tilbury in Essex and Chalk in Kent.

Trans-Pennine Tunnel. This would go under the Pennine Hills between Manchester and Sheffield cutting the journey time between the two cities to just thirty minutes. One option is a road connecting the M67 in the west with the M1 in the east. The tunnel proposed is expected to be eighteen miles long – the longest in Europe.

Other tunnel proposals include a super tunnel under Birmingham City centre and another one under the Irish Sea. Watch this space!

USEFUL WEBSITES

Here are some websites which have connections with road tunnels. Please note that these website links have been provided in good faith. Neither the author nor Hadleigh Books can be held responsible for the functionality and content of these websites.

British Tunnelling Society. The Society aims to promote the art and science of tunnelling by fostering understanding, interest and research in tunnelling. www.britishtunnelling.com

Roads.Org.UK (formerly CRBD – Chris's British Road Directory). This comprehensive website has details of all aspects of the road network of Great Britain, including its tunnels. www.roads.org.uk

Sabre – The Society for All British and Irish Road Enthusiasts. A group of enthusiasts and professionals who discuss roads and share information.
www.sabre-roads.org.uk

Subterranea Britannica – The Society that looks at all aspects of man-made underground structures including tunnels, underground bunkers and mines.
www.subbrit.org.uk

The Road Tunnel Association – A group which represents and promotes the interests of organisations that own and manage road tunnels in the British Isles.
www.rtoa.org.uk

MARK CHATTERTON

About the author

Mark Chatterton first travelled through the Mersey Tunnel (as it was then known) as a baby and from then on he was hooked on road tunnels. In the past ten years or so he has travelled extensively all over Great Britain researching and photographing Britain's road tunnels. This is his first of two books on road tunnels.

MARK CHATTERTON

OTHER TRANSPORT BOOKS

BY MARK CHATTERTON

On the following pages can be found a selection of British road based transport books by Mark Chatterton.

They can be bought from most bookshops or online at:- www.hadleighbooks.co.uk

BRITAIN'S ROAD TUNNELS

This is a more detailed book than *British Road Tunnels – An Introduction*. It looks at every road tunnel to be found in Great Britain whether it be on a motorway, an A-road or in a small street. There are chapters on road tunnels at airports, railway stations and shopping centres. Famous tunnels discussed in the book include the Blackwall Tunnels, the Dartford Tunnels, the Mersey Tunnels and the Hindhead Tunnel. There are approximately 100 colour photographs included as well as a links page.

Printed book ISBN: 9781398100282
E Book ISBN: 9781398100299

Published by Amberley Books

BRITAIN'S MOTORWAYS

This is a more detailed book than *British Motorways - an Introduction*. It looks at every motorway there is in Britain from the M9 and M90 in Scotland right down to the M20 in Kent and the M5 in Devon. It contains detailed entries of almost seventy motorways, as well as over a hundred colour photographs with detailed information on each motorway. There are many other facts and figures about Britain's motorways included including motorways in films, on TV, smart motorways, events which have closed motorways and motorways service stations.

Printed book ISBN: 978139811165
E Book ISBN: 978139811172

Published by Amberley Books

MARK CHATTERTON

BRITISH MOTORWAYS –

AN INTRODUCTION

British Motorways - An Introduction gives the reader a glimpse into the world of motorways in Britain. It looks at famous motorways like the M1, the M6 and the M25, as well as giving details of the longest, widest, shortest and busiest motorways. There are over twenty colour photographs included in the book and also a list of all the motorways in Britain.

Printed book ISBN: 97810811610
E Book ISBN: 97810811603

Published by Hadleigh Books

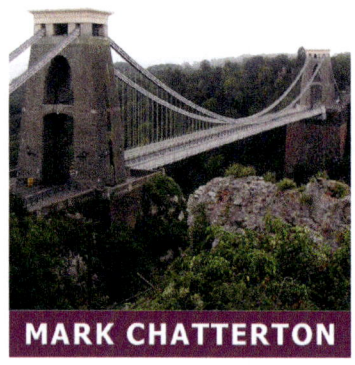

BRITISH ROAD BRIDGES –

AN INTRODUCTION

British Road Bridges - An Introduction gives details of some of the best known road bridges found throughout Great Britain. The book gives details about all the various types of road bridges that are found in Britain, including suspension, bascule and arch bridges. Included are twenty colour photos and background information on each bridge discussed in the book.

Printed book ISBN: 97810811658
E Book ISBN: 97810811641

Published by Hadleigh Books

MARK CHATTERTON

Printed in Great Britain
by Amazon

31673148R00046